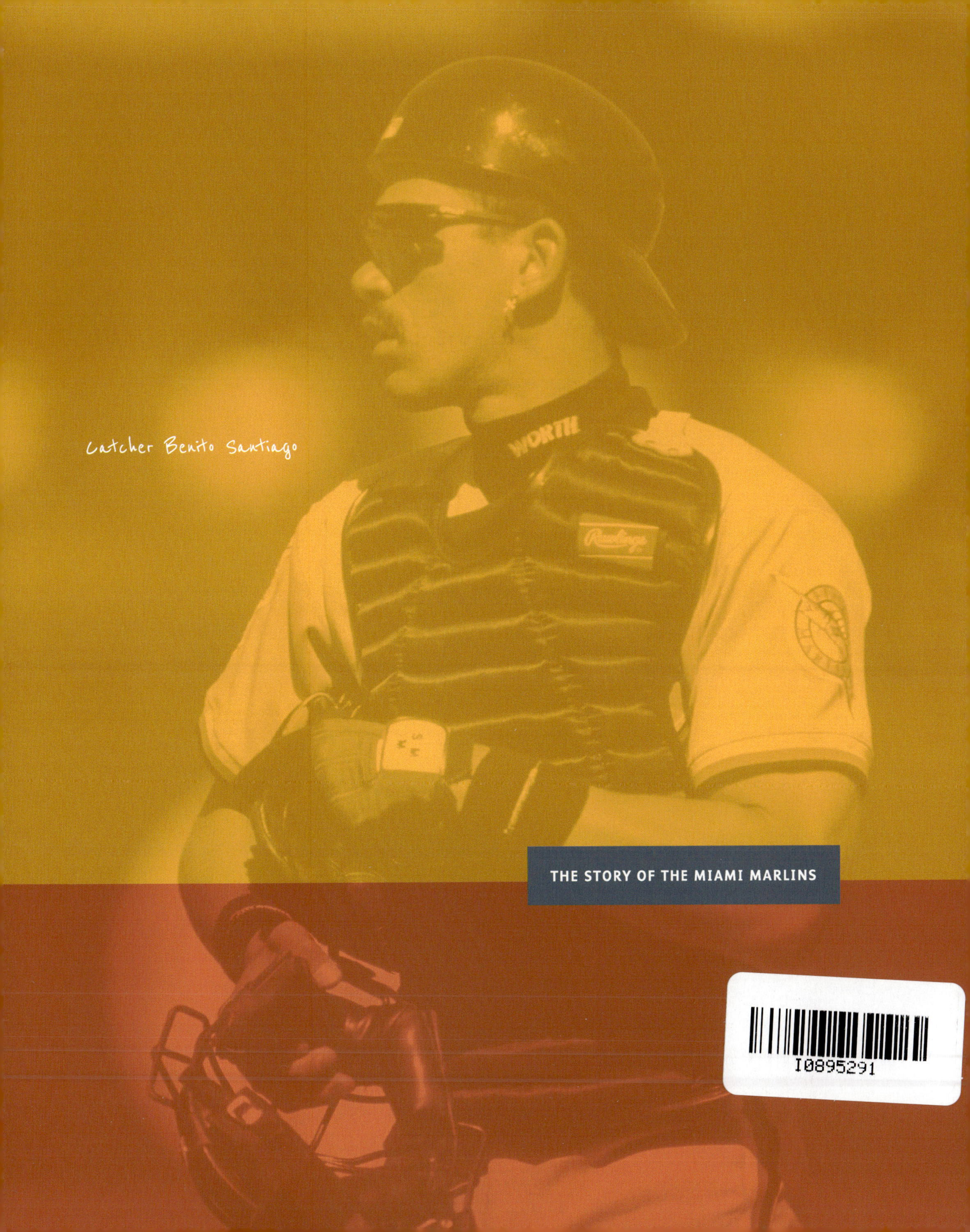

Catcher Benito Santiago

THE STORY OF THE MIAMI MARLINS

The Marlins celebrate after winning the 2003 World Series.

THE STORY OF THE

MIAMI MARLINS

MICHAEL E. GOODMAN

CREATIVE SPORTS

Pitcher Dontrelle Willis

CREATIVE EDUCATION / CREATIVE PAPERBACKS

Published by Creative Education and Creative Paperbacks
P.O. Box 227, Mankato, Minnesota 56002
Creative Education and Creative Paperbacks are imprints of
The Creative Company
www.thecreativecompany.us

Book Design by Graham Morgan
Art direction by Blue Design (www.bluedes.com)

Images by Alamy Stock Photo/Cal Sport Media, 3; Associated Press/Jeffrey Phelps, cover; Getty Images/Bill Smith, 10, Brad Mangin, 23, Bruce Kluckhohn, 24–25, Erick W. Rasco, 2, Focus On Sport, 7 (top, left), 7 (top, right), George Kubas/Diamond Images, 28–29, 31, Jonathan Daniel, 19, Otto Greule Jr, cover, 10, 18, Rich Pilling, 1, 4–5, 6 (top, right), 6 (bottom, left), 7 (bottom, right), 15, 20, 32, Rob Tringali, 30, Ron Vesely, 9, Ronald C. Modra, 16, Scott Boehm, 6 (bottom, right), Scott Wachter/Time Life Pictures, 6 (top, left), Tom Lynn, 7 (bottom, left), 11; Public Domain/12; Wikimedia Commons/Spaluch1, 27

Library of Congress Cataloging-in-Publication Data
Names: Goodman, Michael E. author
Title: The story of the Miami Marlins / by Michael E. Goodman.
Description: Mankato, Minnesota : Creative Education and Creative Paperbacks, [2026] | Series: Creative sports. Major League baseball | Includes index. | Audience: Ages 8-12 | Audience: Grades 4-6 | Summary: "Discover the Miami Marlins' thrilling journey from unexpected World Series wins to recent challenges, featuring legendary players, pivotal moments, and the Major League Baseball team's enduring resilience and determination. Written for middle-grade readers. Includes table of contents, sidebars, and index"– Provided by publisher.
Identifiers: LCCN 2025013110 (print) | LCCN 2025013111 (ebook) | ISBN 9798895810989 library binding | ISBN 9798896800514 paperback | ISBN 9798895812242 ebook
Subjects: LCSH: Miami Marlins (Baseball team)–History–Juvenile literature | Baseball–Florida–History–20th century–Juvenile literature
Classification: LCC GV875.M47 G66 2026 (print) | LCC GV875.M47 (ebook) | DDC 796.357/6409759381–dc23/eng/20250603
LC record available at https://lccn.loc.gov/2025013110
LC ebook record available at https://lccn.loc.gov/2025013111

Printed in the United States

Center fielder Preston Wilson

MARLINS
REDMAN
55
25

19

MARLINS

COUNSELL

CONTENTS

EXTRA INNINGS

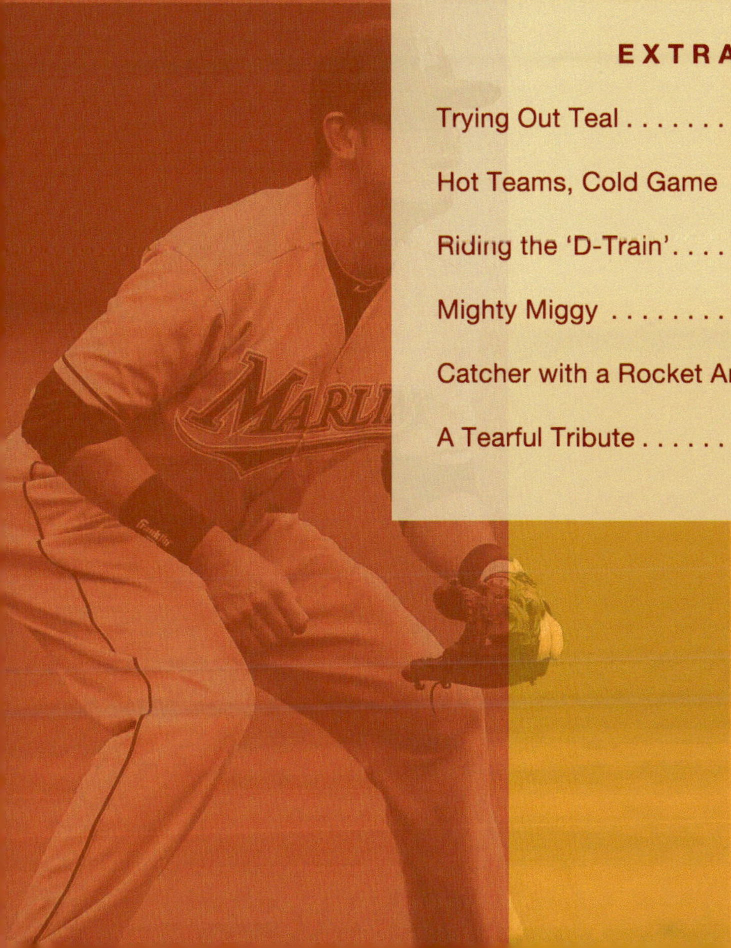

FIRSTS IN FLORIDA

Very few baseball experts expected the Florida Marlins to reach the World Series in 1997. The team was playing in just its fifth season and had posted losing records the first four years. Then, in 1997, the Marlins finished at 92–70 and reached the playoffs for the first time. They won their first two playoff series to earn a World Series berth against the Cleveland Indians.

The Marlins and Indians split the first six World Series games. That set up a Game 7 showdown at Pro Player Stadium in Miami for the 1997 championship. Game 7 was dramatic from the start. The Indians got off to a 2–0 lead. The Marlins scored one run in the seventh on outfielder Bobby Bonilla's home run. They then tied the game on second baseman Craig Counsell's sacrifice fly in the bottom of the ninth. That sent the contest into extra innings. In the bottom of the 11th, Marlins shortstop Édgar Rentería batted with the bases loaded and two outs. He smashed a line drive toward the Cleveland pitcher. The ball tipped off the pitcher's glove and kept going into center field. Counsell, the runner on third base, raced home with the winning run. The Marlins were champions for the first time!

First baseman Jeff Conine

Third baseman Jean Segura

EXTRA INNINGS

Pitcher Charlie Hough

TRYING OUT TEAL

Before the Marlins and Rockies joined the NL in 1993, most teams chose conservative colors for their uniforms and caps. Uniform shirts or caps usually featured red, white, blue, or sometimes gold or orange. The Marlins decided to go with teal as their main color. Teal fit well with the color of the waters off Miami or the color of blue marlins. It also matched the uniform color of the Miami Dolphins in the National Football League, which were also partly owned by Wayne Huizenga. The Rockies were the first team to feature purple as a main color.

Shortstop Édgar Rentería

The Marlins began playing in the National League (NL) in 1993. They were one of two expansion teams added to the league that year. (The Colorado Rockies were the other new NL club.) The first Major League Baseball (MLB) franchise in Florida was awarded to a group from Miami. It was headed by businessman Wayne Huizenga. Huizenga enjoyed deep-sea fishing, especially for blue marlins. So, he named the new franchise the Florida Marlins. "I chose Marlins," he explained, "because the fish is a fierce fighter and adversary that tests your mettle."

Despite the name, the Marlins were not so fierce at first. The club's original roster included mostly aging veterans or young unproven players. The opening day pitcher was 45-year-old knuckleball specialist Charlie Hough. He had grown up in the Miami area. Hough outbattled the Los Angeles Dodgers for a 6–3 win. Then the club lost seven of its next nine games. By season's end, the Marlins' record was 64–98. They finished sixth in the seven-team NL East Division.

Soon, new players joined the lineup in Miami, and the club's record improved each year. Left fielder Jeff Conine became the club's first .300 hitter in 1994. He was named an All-Star that year. Right fielder Gary Sheffield began pounding home runs and driving in runs. In 1996, he totaled 42 homers and 120 runs batted in (RBI) to rank among league leaders. Righty pitching ace Kevin Brown arrived as a free agent before the 1996 season. He won 33

MARLINS
10

games during 1996 and 1997. His wins included a no-hitter and a one-hitter. Relief pitcher Robb Nen was a top closer in the NL. Both hurlers enjoyed pitching to Charles Johnson, one of the best defensive catchers in baseball.

All these players were in place in Miami as the team began its surprising rise in the NL standings during the 1997 season. Led by veteran manager Jim Leyland, the improved Marlins finished just behind the Atlanta Braves in the NL East. They earned the NL Wild Card berth.

In the playoffs, they swept the veteran San Francisco Giants in three games. The powerful Braves were next. The Braves had been NL champions four times since 1991. But they were no match for the Marlins. Brown and rookie pitcher Liván Hernández each won twice, and Florida toppled the Braves in six games.

That set up a confrontation between the Marlins and Indians in the World Series. The teams split the first six games. Then the Marlins made an amazing comeback to win Game 7 in extra innings and earn their first title.

SURVIVING THE 'FIRE SALE'

Florida fans did not have much time to celebrate the club's championship. By Opening Day in 1998, many core players had been traded away. Huizenga explained that the club may have won a title, but it had lost a lot of money. He said he could not afford the team's expensive payroll. The trades became known as the "Florida Fire Sale." (A fire sale involves selling items at heavily discounted prices.) Inexpensive minor-league prospects replaced stars. The team crashed and burned. On the heels of its best season, it had its worst, with 108 losses.

Right fielder Gary Sheffield

The young players began to improve in 1999. "The rest of the league better get ready," warned center fielder Preston Wilson after the season. "Our time is coming soon." Closer Antonio Alfonseca had a breakout season in 2000. He led the majors with 45 saves. Wilson slammed a team-leading 31 homers. Speedy second baseman Luis Castillo led the NL with 62 stolen bases. The Marlins surged to third in the division with a 79–82 record. But they fell back the next two years.

When All-Star catcher Iván Rodríguez joined the team in 2003, he made a prediction. "I think the 2003 season is going to be the year of the Marlins," he said. He was proven right. After a rough start, Florida turned things around. The Marlins ended the season with 91 wins, then a club record.

One key reason for the Marlins' turnaround was the arrival in May of flashy lefty pitcher Dontrelle Willis. On his way to winning NL Rookie of the Year, the "D-Train" won 14 games and struck out 142 batters in just 160 innings.

The Marlins finished the season at 91–71. They became the NL Wild Card team for a second time in their history. And just as they had done in 1997, Florida rolled through the first two playoff rounds. They won the NL pennant and reached the World Series. Their opponents were the powerful New York Yankees, winners of four World Series titles between 1996 and 2000.

Florida fans were excited about the matchup with the Yankees. "How great is it that a fairly new team has been able to go to the series twice in the past six years and others haven't been able to in decades?" said native New Yorker Steven Burgos, who now lived in Florida. Fans were not the only ones who were excited. "This is my first time [as a manager in the World Series]," Miami skipper Jack McKeon said. "It is probably the biggest moment of my professional career. I can't even explain it. It hasn't even sunk in yet."

Florida took Game 1. The Yankees won the next two. Game 4 stretched to 12 innings. Finally, shortstop Alex González homered to win the contest, 4–3.

EXTRA INNINGS

PITCHER LIVAN HERNANDEZ

HOT TEAMS, COLD GAME

The Marlins hosted the first two games of the 1997 World Series in Miami. It was sunny and warm. The next three games took place at Jacobs Field in Cleveland. Game 4 was the coldest World Series game on record. With windchill, the temperature was a frigid 18 degrees Fahrenheit. Snowflakes swirled in the air. Players wore long underwear and turtlenecks. They had gloves on their throwing hands. Bats snapped like brittle toothpicks. Fielders and base runners had trouble keeping their footing. The Indians won, 10–3. Marlins' president Don Smiley said, "I love hunting ducks in October, and today was the Super Bowl of duck-hunting weather."

EXTRA INNINGS

DONTRELLE WILLIS
PITCHER
MARLINS SEASONS: 2003–07
6-FOOT-2, 230 POUNDS
KEY STATS: NL ROOKIE OF THE YEAR 2003
PLAYED IN 2 ALL-STAR GAMES (2003, 2005)
TOSSED 5 SHUTOUTS IN 2005
LED NL WITH 22 WINS IN 2005

RIDING THE D-TRAIN

By age 12, Dontrelle ("D-Train") Willis had developed his unique pitching style. He kicked his right leg higher than his head. His back briefly faced the batter. Then the ball appeared. It looked like it was coming out of his shirt. Willis won 14 games in 2003. He was named NL Rookie of the Year. He was even better two years later. He finished second in voting for the NL Cy Young Award. After the 2007 season, the Marlins traded him to Detroit. But he left a lasting legacy. "He's just a guy you love to be around," said a teammate. "He'd always find a way to make you smile."

In Game 5, the Marlins held off the Yankees to win 6–4. McKeon then sent flame-throwing righthander Josh Beckett to the mound for Game 6. Beckett was irked by the media's constant reminders of the Yankees' championship tradition. "All I knew," he said, "was that WE were going to get World Series rings on Opening Day next season."

Beckett backed up his words. He tossed a complete-game shutout. The Marlins won, 2–0, to capture their second title. It was one of the biggest upsets in World Series history.

NEW HOME, NEW NAME

Unfortunately, the team's playoff magic spell didn't last very long. The Marlins posted winning records in four of the next six seasons. But they kept falling short of reaching the postseason again. Fans still had a lot to cheer about in those years. Florida sent four players to the 2004 All-Star Game. One was the club's newest star, outfielder Miguel Cabrera.

Cabrera had joined the Marlins in 2003. He played a key role in Florida's World Series win that year, smacking a dramatic home run in Game 4. He was named an All-Star the next four years. During those years, he batted over .300 three times and averaged 32 home runs and 115 RBI per season. Before the 2008 season, Cabrera and Dontrelle Willis were traded to Detroit for six of the Tigers' top prospects. Sadly, the new Marlins never really succeeded in Florida. Meanwhile, Cabrera went on to become one of the biggest stars in the

American League (AL) for the next 16 years. Miami fans have always regretted losing "Miggy."

Cabrera was joined in the Marlins lineup by shortstop Hanley Ramírez from the Dominican Republic. Ramírez earned NL Rookie of the Year honors in 2006. Then he batted over .300 for four straight seasons for Florida. He played in three All-Star Games. In 2009, he won the NL batting crown with a .342 average.

The Marlins best pitchers during this rebuilding period were righthanders Josh Johnson and Aníbal Sánchez. Johnson was named an All-Star in 2009 and 2010. In 2010, he topped the league with a 2.30 ERA (earned run average). In 2011, Sánchez recorded 202 strikeouts, sixth best in the league.

The Marlins had been lucky bringing up young players so far in their history. All-Star shortstop Édgar Rentería had been only 19 when he arrived in Miami in 1996. Miguel Cabrera was just two months past his 20th birthday when he joined the Marlins in 2003. So, in 2010, Florida leaders decided to promote another "baby," 20-year-old Giancarlo Stanton. At 6-foot-6 and 245 pounds, Stanton was a very big and powerful baby. He began flexing his muscles right away. He went 3-for-5 and scored twice in his debut game. Then, he smacked a mammoth grand slam a few games later.

One home run Stanton hit later in the season stayed in his memory. Batting against Phillies star pitcher Roy Oswalt, Stanton thought he had struck out. But the catcher dropped the ball. Given a second chance, Stanton slammed the next pitch into the stands.

"That one I really liked because that's what made me grow," Stanton said. "I thought I struck out; I was a little flustered." But he didn't give up. He put that lesson to work many times in the next few years when the Marlins continued to play well but still miss the playoffs.

In 2012, the team moved to its new home, Marlins Park. The stadium featured a retractable (closeable) roof to protect against summer heat and

Pitcher Josh Johnson

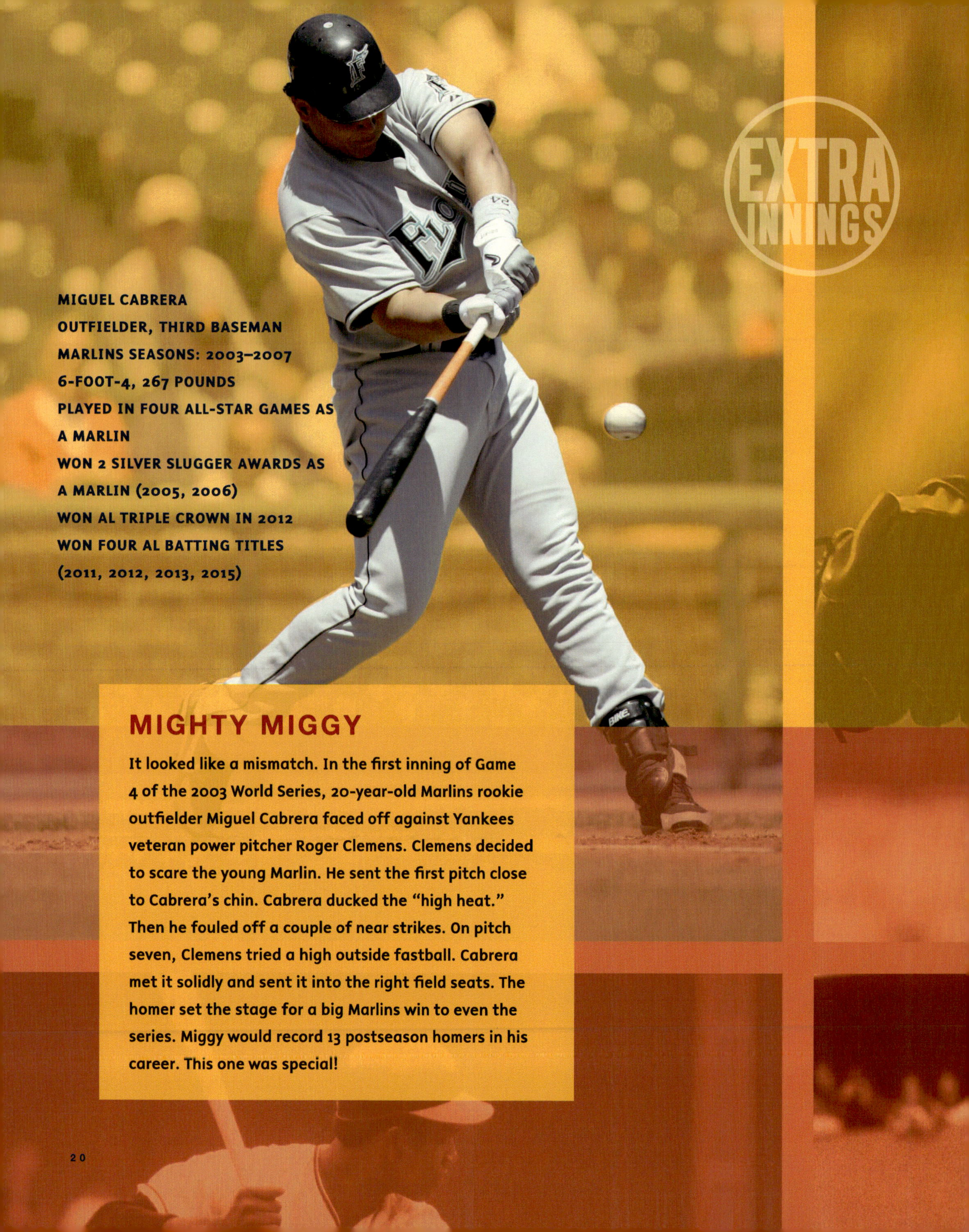

EXTRA INNINGS

MIGUEL CABRERA
OUTFIELDER, THIRD BASEMAN
MARLINS SEASONS: 2003–2007
6-FOOT-4, 267 POUNDS
PLAYED IN FOUR ALL-STAR GAMES AS A MARLIN
WON 2 SILVER SLUGGER AWARDS AS A MARLIN (2005, 2006)
WON AL TRIPLE CROWN IN 2012
WON FOUR AL BATTING TITLES (2011, 2012, 2013, 2015)

MIGHTY MIGGY

It looked like a mismatch. In the first inning of Game 4 of the 2003 World Series, 20-year-old Marlins rookie outfielder Miguel Cabrera faced off against Yankees veteran power pitcher Roger Clemens. Clemens decided to scare the young Marlin. He sent the first pitch close to Cabrera's chin. Cabrera ducked the "high heat." Then he fouled off a couple of near strikes. On pitch seven, Clemens tried a high outside fastball. Cabrera met it solidly and sent it into the right field seats. The homer set the stage for a big Marlins win to even the series. Miggy would record 13 postseason homers in his career. This one was special!

rain. Miami-Dade County provided much of the financing. As part of the deal, the team's official name became the Miami Marlins. The changes did not help on the field, however. The club won just 69 games that year. But they did draw 700,000 more fans than the year before. When the Marlins went 62–100 in 2013, it was clear that changes were needed.

STRIVING FOR STABILITY

For much of their history, the Marlins kept making changes. Favorite players were traded away. Managers were replaced after a short time. With the new stadium in place, team management hoped to create a more stable environment in Miami. One of the first steps was to lock the team's top star, Giancarlo Stanton, into a long-term contract. In 2014, Stanton signed one of the largest contracts so far in the history of professional sports: $325 million over 13 years. Stanton responded by smacking a league-leading 37 homers that season. Injuries plagued the big slugger the next two years. Then he broke out in a big way in 2017. His 59 home runs and 132 RBI topped the major leagues.

While Stanton was the team's batting star, young righty José Fernández shone bright on the mound. The big Cuban righthander joined the Marlins as a 20-year-old in 2013. He compiled a 12–6 record his first season. He made the All-Star team and earned Rookie of the Year honors. He quickly became a hero to South Florida's Cuban community. Fernández was injured for most of the next two seasons. He overcame his injuries to win 16 games in 2016 and made his second All-Star team. Tragically, Fernández died in a boating accident in late September of 2016. Miami fans were stunned. "He was one of our game's

Pitcher José Fernández

great young stars who made a dramatic impact on and off the field since his debut in 2013," said MLB Commissioner Rob Manfred.

Stanton's outstanding season in 2017 buoyed fans' hope for a brighter future in Miami. But the optimism soon faded when team management decided it could not afford Stanton's big contract anymore. Efforts to renegotiate the contract failed. Fearing that Stanton might decide to become a free agent, the Marlins traded him to the Yankees. Without him, the team lost momentum. It won just 63 games in 2018. The Marlins were even worse in 2019. Their 57 wins was the lowest total in the NL.

Two former Yankees greats then stepped in to try to rebuild the club. Don Mattingly was a top hitter and fielder during his playing career in New York. He took over as team manager in 2016. He remained in that role for seven seasons. Fellow Yankee, Hall of Fame shortstop Derek Jeter, was part of the group that bought the club in 2017. He became chief executive officer (CEO), in charge of business matters. Both men played important roles when the Marlins made a surprise run to the playoffs in 2020.

Because of the COVID pandemic, the 2020 season was shortened to 60 games. The Marlins went 31–29 to finish second in the NL East. They earned a Wild Card spot. Led on offense by third baseman Brian Anderson and on the mound by righthander Sandy Alcántara, the Marlins reached the second round of the playoffs. Then they were eliminated by the Atlanta Braves. The loss hurt, but Marlins' fans believed that the team was on the right track again.

Pitcher Sandy Alcántara

Miami
Rawlings

CHARLES JOHNSON
CATCHER
MARLINS SEASONS: 1994–98, 2001–02
6-FOOT-2, 215 POUNDS
WON FOUR CONSECUTIVE GOLD GLOVES (1995–98)
PLAYED IN TWO ALL-STAR GAMES
TOPPED THE NL BY THROWING OUT 56 RUNNERS IN 1997
THREW OUT MORE THAN 40 PERCENT OF BASE STEALERS IN 7 SEASONS

EXTRA INNINGS

CATCHER WITH A ROCKET ARM

Charles Johnson won the Gold Glove award as the best fielding catcher in the NL in 1995, his first full MLB season. He won the award in the next three seasons, too. He was an All-Star in 1997. That same year, he went the entire season without committing an error. Johnson left Florida in 1998 for the Los Angeles Dodgers. He returned three years later and was selected as an All-Star again in 2001. That season, he agreed to donate $100 to a charity each time he threw out a base stealer. He sent a check for $3,700 to the charity after the season.

HOPING FOR MIAMI MAGIC

After the Marlins finally reached the playoffs again in 2020, Miami fans began dreaming that a third World Series title would soon be in the club's future. Then the club went through two more losing campaigns.

While the team's record in 2022 was poor, one star had a very successful year. Pitcher Sandy Alcántara led the NL with 228 innings pitched. He also struck out more than 200 batters for the second time in his career. Baseball writers rewarded his efforts by unanimously voting him the 2022 Cy Young Award winner. He became the first Miami pitcher to receive the honor.

Following the season, Mattingly was let go after seven years. He served 1,030 games as team manager, 500 more than any previous skipper. Jeter also decided to leave his management position. He complained that the club's tight budgets had made it too hard to improve the team.

A new manager, Skip Schumaker, came in with high expectations in 2023. He lived up to those expectations in his first year at the helm. He pushed the Marlins' players to an 84–78 record. That was good enough to earn another Wild Card berth into the postseason. It also impressed writers enough to choose him as NL Manager of the Year.

Miami fans were thrilled by the team's progress. They especially enjoyed watching lefty-hitting second baseman Luis Arraez slash hits to all parts of the LoanDepot park. (That became the new official name of Marlins Park in 2021.) Arraez finished the season with an NL best .354 average. Amazingly, Arraez had led the AL in batting with the Minnesota Twins the previous year.

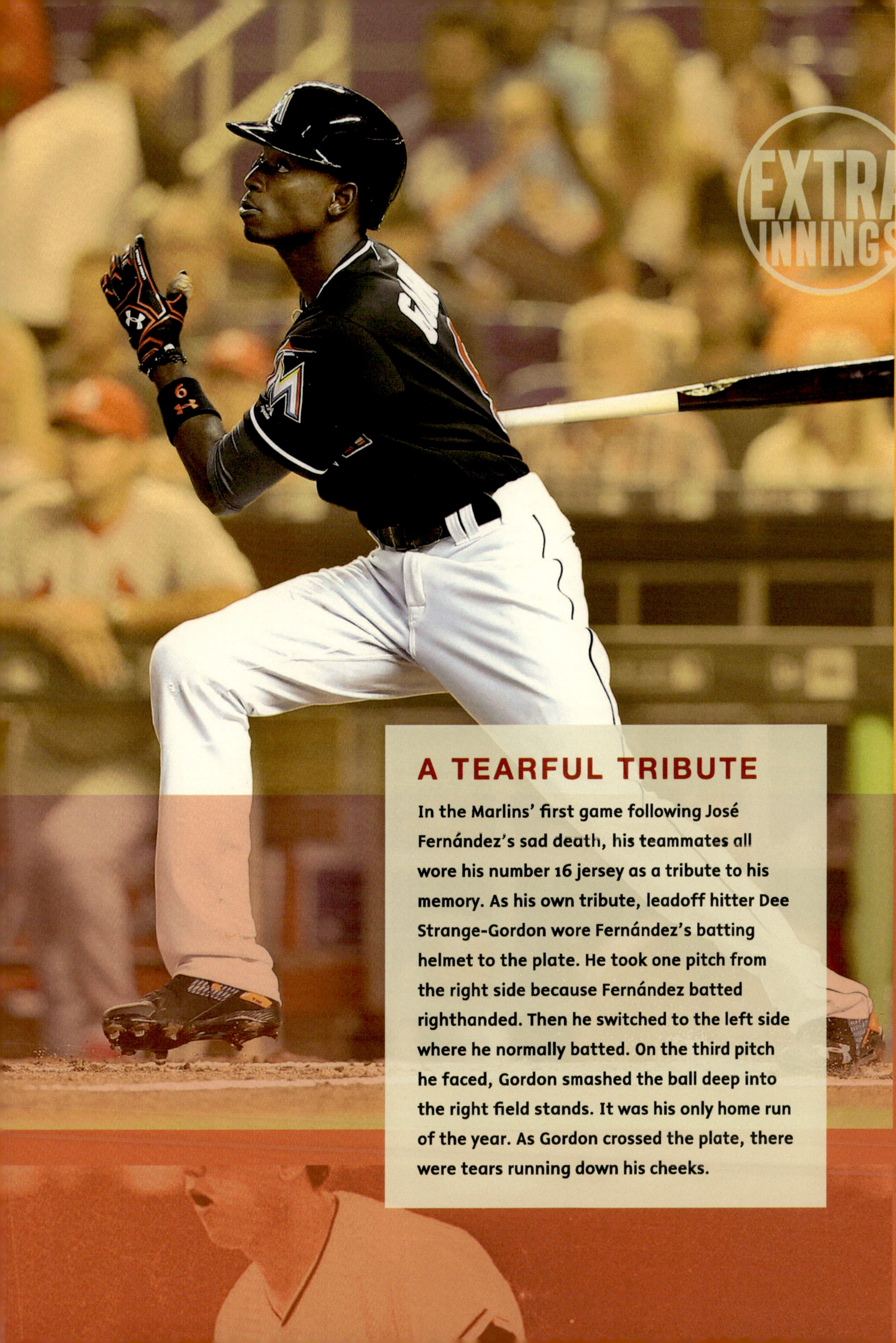

EXTRA INNINGS

A TEARFUL TRIBUTE

In the Marlins' first game following José Fernández's sad death, his teammates all wore his number 16 jersey as a tribute to his memory. As his own tribute, leadoff hitter Dee Strange-Gordon wore Fernández's batting helmet to the plate. He took one pitch from the right side because Fernández batted righthanded. Then he switched to the left side where he normally batted. On the third pitch he faced, Gordon smashed the ball deep into the right field stands. It was his only home run of the year. As Gordon crossed the plate, there were tears running down his cheeks.

Pitcher Max Meyers

He is the only player in baseball history to win a batting title in the American and National Leagues in consecutive seasons.

Unfortunately, Miami was quickly eliminated by the Philadelphia Phillies in the first round of the playoffs. So fans would have to wait longer to celebrate another World Series title.

The Marlins took a step back in 2024, and Arraez and several other team veterans were traded away for a group of promising young players. The new prospects provide hope for a better future in Miami.

Schumaker also decided to leave after the season. He was replaced by former Dodgers coach Clayton McCullough. Marlins president Peter Bendix said he was certain the team had picked the right man to lead the club into a positive future. "Clayton knows the importance of people and the importance of building a winning culture. . . . We want to build something that is successful every single year, year in and year out. I think Clayton can be the right leader for that."

In their short but rocky history, the Miami Marlins have given fans two electrifying World Series wins. The fans have been patient. They eagerly await the day when the "Fighting Fish" reel in another title for South Florida.

Shortstop Xavier Edwards

INDEX